Momma,
How Long Will You
Love Me?

Debra Downey

To order additional copies of this book, contact:
Xlibris
1-888-795-4274
www.Xlibris.com
Orders@Xlibris.com

Foreword

Mothers and daughters seem to go through phases and stages in their love for each other. It seems to revolve and evolve and comes full circle. In the end it doesn't matter all that much, as the love a mother and daughter have for each other is special and eternal!

Dedication

This book is dedicated to, and was written for Amber my firstborn daughter who so closely resembles these verses.

It is also dedicated to my youngest daughter who happened along eleven years later, and not surprisingly, also closely resembles the verses.

Once, when you were five, you asked me in your sweet little girl voice, momma how long will you love me?

I happily replied, until the very, very last good night!

Then, when you were ten, you asked me in your big girl voice, how long will you love me momma?

This time I lovingly replied. Until the very end of time.

When you were thirteen, once, and only once, in your new teenaged, sophisticated voice, you shyly asked me this. Momma, how long will you love me?

I quietly and quickly replied. Until, and even long after, you forget to, or stop asking me, and all the rivers run dry.

At sixteen when you asked me in a sarcastic, to cool to care voice, momma how long will you love me now?

I sadly, and with tears in my eyes replied. I will love you until the day I die!

Every night after, eagerly, I waited for you to ask me: momma how long will you love me?!

But you forgot to ask me and I never asked you why.

And I waited

And waited!

Then, after many, many years went by, on the day of your wedding, you surprised me by asking me, with tears in your eyes:

Momma how long will you love me?

And to this I ecstatically replied:

Until the heavens open up and swallow the sky.

Until the very, very last goodnight!!!

Until the the very end of time!!!

Until the rivers all run dry!

Until, and even long, long after I die!!!!

Printed in the United States
By Bookmasters